London Bridge Station

HORSE OMNIBUS

Entertaining and instructive episodes
from the history of its horses
and the manners of its men

by

ROY SHADWELL

PETER WOOLLER

1. The Birth of the Omnibus

If you define a bus service as a timed service on a fixed route for fare-paying passengers, then the first bus service started in the far off days of 1662! The Carrosses à cinq sols (roughly translated as the 5d carriage) were the brain child of Blaise Pascal, the French philosopher who, not being wealthy enough to put his scheme into action, turned to his friend the Duc de Roannes, for financial help. The Duc, impressed with the idea, immediately set up a company and persuaded fellow aristocrats to take out shares. Equally important, he obtained a decree from Louis XIV authorising the establishment of the company.

Seven coaches, to carry eight inside passengers, were built and at 7 a.m. on March 18th, 1662, the world's first horse bus service was launched with due ceremony.

Large crowds gathered to witness the start. Two Commissaires of the Châtelet, dressed in official robes and attended by City Archers and a troop of cavalry, performed the opening ceremony. After extolling the service as a boon to the general public, the officials gave dire warnings to any who were tempted to interfere with the service or set up in opposition. The King himself would punish anyone interfering with the coaches, their drivers or conductors; and as for unauthorised competitors, they would be fined 3,000 francs and their coaches and horses confiscated! The Commissaires then presented each crew a long blue coat with the Royal Arms and City Arms embroidered in brilliant colours and gave the command for the service to commence. The party split in two, one Commissaire and half the retinue going to the Luxembourg terminus and the rest to the Porte St. Antoine. The two coaches set off – empty, despite the waiting crowds – an unprofessional start that boded ill for the future.

At first the service was a roaring success – if success is filling seats. At the beginning of every journey there was an unseemly rush to be seated, manners were forgotten, many a Parisian frock was ruined.

Carrosses à cinq sols were the latest fashion, a fashion which spread outwards to the suburbs. Suburban Parisians flocked to see the new vehicles, though few managed to get a ride, for the rush became daily greater. And to add to the excitement the King himself took a ride in one of the coaches. Where the King led, the wealthy and aristocracy followed. Many arrived at the terminus in their own private carriages and jostled with the poorer classes to obtain seats. They returned day after day for up to a fortnight until at last they obtained a ride!

Success seemed guaranteed, four other routes started within as many months, but success founded upon the whims of fashion is doomed. The fascination and aura of respectability started to wane and with them the passengers. The middle classes decided that it was quicker to walk, while soldiers, pages, lackeys and others in uniform were forbidden to ride 'for the greater convenience of people of merit!'

left:"Let's all go down the Strand!" (1890s)

As Pascal died the year his coaches started he did not live to see his dream crumbling, his coaches starting to run half empty and then without passengers at all. After his death the sevice continued for some years but every month the clientele dwindled and it was only a question of time before the carrosses would run no more. A potentially useful method of conveying people had been turned by the vagaries of fashion into something ressembling a novel ride on a fairground.

150 years later Paris was ready to try again. Some authors suggest that in 1819 the banker and politician Jacques Lafitte started public transport in Paris, while others claim that his application to start such a service was turned down for fear of traffic jams.

It was in another French city, Nantes, that the 'omnibus' first appeared. Stanislaus Baudry, formerly a colonel under the Empire, opened some hot water baths in the suburb of Richebourg, and in 1825 commenced a service of public carriages to serve them. The first ones bore the legend 'Voitures de Richebourg', but their Nantes terminus was outside the hat shop of Monsieur Omnes, who used his name for a Latin pun on his shop sign 'Omnes Omnibus'. This was much appreciated by the populace, and Baudry borrowed part of the title for his vehicles.

He soon found that people were using his omnibuses simply as a means of transport and not for visiting his baths, so he turned his attention to Paris where, this time, authorisation was forthcoming, and in 1828 he opened ten routes served by 100 omnibuses. The vehicles carried 14 passengers.

Such was their success that several rival firms took to the streets, and this competition, coupled with the harsh winter of 1829 with its escalating forage bills and almost impassable streets, caused Baudry to fear bankruptcy. He took the suicide's way out, in the Canal St. Martin. A sad end for the man who gave us the term which we still use today in its shortened form, bus.

An ironic end, too – his firm recovered and carried on. So did some of the others.

Meanwhile, with the spate of omnibus construction in Paris, an expatriot Englishman, George Shillibeer, started to ply his trade as a carriage builder, an art he had learnt with Hatchett's of Long Acre after leaving the Royal Navy as a midshipman (serving on the *San Josef* and the *Royal George*). Fashion again played her card with rather better results than before, for English carriages were deemed the height of elegance. Shillibeer prospered, so much so that Jacques Lafitte commissioned him to build luxury omnibuses of novel design. Shillibeer then recrossed the Channel, inspired to bring the omnibus to London. He set up his new enterprise in Bury Street, Bloomsbury and made it known to one and all that he intended to operate an omnibus service. The word 'omnibus' received a mixed reception:

"If one vehicle is called an omnibus, what are two or more called?"

"Omnibuses," replied Shillibeer promptly. However, most people referred to them as omnis or Shillibeers.

The new service was to run, appropriately enough, along the New Road, as

Marylebone Road, Euston Road and Pentonville Road were then known, between the Yorkshire Stingo (a renowned public house) at Paddington and Bank. The route itself was not new; three or four short-stage coaches had been operating it in sections for many years, but the journey took three hours and it was expensive, 2/- for outside passengers, and 3/- for those wanting comfort inside. Shillibeer's new omnibus would make the journey cheaper (1/-) as well as quicker. He was poised to provide robust competition.

Shillibeer's first omnibus

2. Shillibeer's Omnibuses take the Road

Shillibeer's service started on the morning of July 4th, 1829, witnessed by a large gathering of onlookers.

The Omnibus was built to carry 22 inside passengers (although some sources say 18) and was drawn by three magnificent bays harnessed abreast. A second vehicle soon joined the first (August 1st has been quoted, though some historians suggest the service had two vehicles from the outset. Shillibeer's own advertisement implies one, doing five return trips daily) With two omnibuses an hourly service was worked, with 12 trips a day, bringing in about £100 a week in fares. Shillibeer's enterprise was certainly proving a success.

Almost as successful and interesting as the vehicles were Shillibeer's two conductors. Both were sons of naval officers and, having lived in Paris, they were fluent in French as well as being familiar with the duties of a conductor.There was opposition from some of the short-stage coach proprietors who played the xenophobic card, saying that Shillibeer should not be allowed to run his French vehicles in England. Some residents of Paddington Green were also against the enterprise, saying that the Green would be doomed if the omnibuses continued to run – but opposition from the householders did not deter their daughters from travelling to King's Cross and back again regularly – ostensibly to improve their French by conversing with the young gentlemen from Paris! However, the young ladies' French lessons were short lived. The cosmopolitan conductors were soon replaced by paid staff.

The new conductors, while emulating the manners of their French predecessors, were easily tempted into the sin of thinking themselves more deserving of money than their employer and pocketing some fares. Takings decreased daily while the number of passengers remained unchanged, at least according to the people who lived along the route. Shillibeer was forced into taking action to discover the reason for the downturn in his fortunes. He planted people whom he could trust as spies on the omnibuses. These first inspectors discovered that between them the two conductors were robbing Shillibeer of about £20 a week. A princely sum for those days. And, having stolen it, they could not resist spending it. It took no Sherlock Holmes to deduce from where the funds came for champagne suppers for themselves and their friends at the Yorkshire Stingo. And the champagne loosened their tongues, they bragged of the source of their easy money – £10 each a week over and above their legitimate wages of 10/-. But Shillibeer's spies also frequented the Yorkshire Stingo. With evidence such as this Shillibeer took the obvious action and dismissed the conductors. But would their replacements survive temptation any better? A better solution must be found.

The problem seemed solved when Shillibeer was approached by an inventor with a 'register', a device that fitted underneath the bus, attached to the step. Everytime anyone entered the omnibus they stood on a plate and were counted mechanically. The device seemed foolproof and Shillibeer ordered one at a cost of £300, insisting that its inventor acted as conductor while it proved its worth. For a fortnight the device worked as intended but friends of the sacked conductors sought revenge. They smashed the patent device with a sledgehammer – nearly killing its hapless inventor. Shillibeer had no intention of letting another £300 go the same way. Instead he introduced a less expensive check that was used in Paris. A specially made clock was placed in a prominent position with a notice nearby informing passengers that it was the conductor's duty to move the pointer on every time a passenger boarded. Conductors who failed to do this, said the notice, should be reported to the proprietor. However, not one report was ever made; indeed the passengers delighted in moving the pointer themselves – making the omnibus carry seemingly impossible loads! This made a nonsense of the pointer's purpose. Nonetheless, Shillibeer went from strength to strength. Within nine months he had 12 omnibuses at work. Of course it took longer to solve the question of fares, and the steps that were taken will be revealed later in these pages.

Right: Shillibeer's third omnibus, boldly inscribed with his name. Others emulated him

3. Competition ... and the Law

In 1832, in the face of competition, and with the hope of increasing his fleet, Shillibeer took a Mr. William Morton, a Southwell publican into partnership. Two years later the partnership split. Morton took as his share the whole of the original New Rd. route, a route on which there was no competition. However, without Shillibeer he failed to make even this line pay. Morton fell on hard times and was eventually forced to seek work as a conductor. But even in this he was a failure and was sacked for drunkenness. In a spell of depression he committed suicide at his lodgings in Little Castle St. off Edgware Rd.

At the inquest Shillibeer's competitors tried to hold him responsible for Morton's death, claiming that he had swindled the unfortunate man, but Shillibeer's generosity in giving Morton the New Rd. route proved the opposite. Morton's mismanagement was found to be the root cause of his misfortunes – the man to whom he had sold the New Rd. route made it pay handsomely.

Short-stage coach proprietors eventually realised that omnibuses were a better prospect than coaches and became Shillibeer's competitors instead of his antagonists, but he had the advantage of an established reputation which kept him in the forefront. Some of the newcomers had the cheek to paint 'Shillibeer' on the sides of their omnibuses. Shillibeer countered by renaming his vehicles 'Shillibeer's Original Omnibuses.'

However, they were not content merely to emulate Shillibeer, they wanted to go one better. One competitor made all his drivers put a wooden ring on each arm. The rings were attached to strings which went the full length of the ceiling. Passengers had merely to pull one string or the other to tell the driver on which side they wanted to dismount. This arrangement with strings was so popular with customers that strong letters of complaint were sent to proprietors without such a system! The Metropolitan Street Act of 1867, however, required omnibuses to pick up and set down passengers as near as possible to the left of the street, or risk a fine of 40/-.

One competitor, a Mr. Cloud, outshone Shillibeer for a while. He operated possibly the first library bus service which ran between the White Horse, Haymarket, Chelsea and Hammersmith. Newspapers were standard on Shillibeer's buses but Mr. Cloud lined his omnibuses with bookshelves stocked with works by popular authors of the day. Then as now books were expensive and some people travelled to Hammersmith and back merely to read the latest books. It is not hard to imagine what put an end to such a service – books provided for the common good ended up in private pockets. Frustrated and disgusted, Mr. Cloud publicly announced that dishonesty on the part of his patrons had forced him to discontinue the library buses.

It might be thought that the London of 150 years ago had few traffic problems but this was not the case. An Act of Parliament empowered the police to apprehend any driver of a public vehicle who refused to move on when instructed so to do. Some of the omnibuses were loitering at Hammersmith, no doubt hoping to pick up additional passengers before starting off, or perhaps enjoying an extended morning break, the licensing laws were less strict then. One morning two drivers were pulled from their boxes and taken to the local police station. The next day the courts fined them 40/-, or a month in prison. For a few days it seemed that the law had triumphed but one Saturday evening, a loitering omnibus brought the traffic in Knightsbridge to a standstill. A policeman commanded the driver to move on but he refused. Two policemen dashed forward to pull him from his seat, but found to their amazement that he was chained to his seat! The chain was secured with a large padlock. As the policemen stood dumbfounded, wondering what to do, several more omnibuses pulled up, their drivers likewise immobilised. A large crowd gathered, much amused at the sight of omnibus drivers rattling their chains in defiance at the law. Having proved their point they moved on, only to be fined a few days later.

The attitude of the police at the new Act can only be guessed at but the shopkeepers had no doubts. They wanted the streets kept clear so that their wealthy customers could pull up to the door of their shops in private carriages. One aptly named Mr. Shufflebottom, a silk merchant of Ludgate Hill, was strong in his resolve to stop omnibuses loitering. He applied for summonses against 24 conductors. All were fined.

However, public opinion soon turned the tables; it became more difficult for shopkeepers to obtain summonses. On one occasion an alderman had before him no less than 120 conductors who had committed the sin of stopping outside shops when a carriage was waiting to pull in. He discharged every one of them. His decision was popular. It was ludicrous that private coaches carrying no more than four people should take precedence over vehicles carrying six times that number. In 1832, the Stage Carriage Act came into force. Now at last public vehicles were given the right to pick up and set down passengers on the streets of London without prejudice.

Stage coach and omnibus, Leadenhall St. 1831

4. The Fate of Shillibeer

Shillibeer was still centre stage in the omnibus world but was now setting his sights further afield. He gave up his metropolitan business soon after the partnership with Morton was dissolved and started running omibuses between London, Greenwich and Woolwich, putting 20 vehicles on the route. This was a brave step to take. Plans were already well advanced for a railway service to serve the same ends. He was perhaps over ambitious in thinking that he could compete with a railway. He was encouraged by the widespread opinion that he would see off any competition from the railways, his plans even inspired a popular song, but this time his business sense had failed him. Shillibeer's Original Omnibuses proved no match for the railway. As soon as the railway service was started in 1835 his takings fell off. He struggled on but it was a losing battle. He got into arrears with the Stamp and Tax Offices, they seized his omnibuses and would not let him operate until the money was paid – a nonsensical stance to take towards a debtor. This happened three or four times and compounded the reasons for failure – with each interruption of the service more passengers defected to the railways. Acting on advice, Shillibeer appealed to the Lords of the Treasury for compensation. Shortly afterwards he was offered the post of Assistant Registrar of Licenses, a post created by the newly passed Bill for the regulation of omnibuses in and near the Metropolis. He refused, believing that he had been promised the top position.

This second omnibus Act of 1838 made it mandatory that the words 'Metropolitan Stage Carriage' together with the Stamp Office number and numbers of passengers, be displayed on each omnibus both outside and within. Moreover each driver and conductor was to wear a numbered badge so that they could be readily identified by the public and the police in case of misconduct.

Shillibeer continued to press for compensation for damage to his business done at the hands of the Stamp and Tax office. His name was put forward for several other posts but he obtained none. Likewise his claim, though never disputed, was ignored. Losing faith in Government promises he decided that life as a civil servant was not for him.

Shillibeer put the world of the omnibus behind him and changed career yet again, becoming an undertaker. He set up premises next to Bunhill Fields burial ground and established a successful business which he ran until his death. Were it not for this last change of profession we might still be calling buses 'Shillibeers' in the same way that Hansom became a popular synonym for a cab. But once his hearses became a common sight on the streets of London, people were understandably reluctant to say that they were going to take a Shillibeer and the term omnibus prevailed.

Shillibeer died in Brighton on August 22nd, 1866 at the age of 69. It is sad that he is so little remembered today and has no lasting memorial, for in introducing his omnibuses he brought a cheap and convenient mode of transport to all.

5. A Potential Rival: Steam

Though Shillibeer abandoned road passenger transport and Baudry drowned himself in despair, the horse omnibus itself continued to prosper. This, however, was not to be the destiny of a potentially viable alternative, the steam road-carriage. As early as 1769, when Joseph Cugnot, a French military engineer, put a steam-driven three-wheel tractor on the road, many such experiments were made, and by the early 1820s several British engineers were designing steam vehicles and taking out patents. Among the most successful was Sir Goldsworthy Gurney. His steam carriage of 1827 did the London to Bath run at an average of 15 m.p.h. (stage coaches did no better than 10 m.p.h.). Its body was that of a stage coach, on a lengthened chassis, with 'Royal Patent' in bold letters on its side. It is also said to have made many journeys in London in the next two years, but these may not have been on normal revenue services. He constructed further vehicles, with several very

Gurney's 1827 steam carriage speeding past an inn. Landlords feared for lost trade

necessary improvements; one of them was attacked by what we would now call Luddites in 1829. In 1831 the coaches were taken over by Sir Charles Dance who commenced a thrice daily service between Gloucester and Cheltenham. In four months this carried 3,000 passengers, but then Dance was forced off the road by local opposition.

Meanwhile, again in 1827, Walter Hancock patented a remarkaby efficient boiler, and this, with various subsequent experiments, resulted in his starting a service between Stratford (Essex) and London, with a steam carriage called 'The Infant', in 1831.

Later he ran larger steam carriages, the 'Era' and the 'Autopsy' in direct competition with Shillibeer's omnibuses on the Yorkshire Stingo-Bank route. Steam carriages were faster and cheaper than the omnibus, they were fully in keeping with the Victorian quest for modernity, and a great future was forecast. The 'Era' carried 14 passengers who were charged 6d apiece. To achieve a speed of 10 m.p.h. the steam carriage consumed eight to ten pounds of coke and a hundred pounds of water per mile.

Steam carriages had the additional advantage of good brakes and an efficient steering system – at least in their inventors' view. Horses have a will of their own and in London's crowded streets it was sometimes difficult for horse bus drivers to avoid collisions. However, a better safety record and the Victorian enthusiasm for mechanical transport were not enough to ensure the steamers' success. They

Hancock rush hour! 'Autopsy', 'Era' and 'Infant'

broke down with monotonous regularity and the time spent in roadside repairs would have infuriated the modern commuter, although perhaps London's suburban population had more patience in those days.

Everyone assured themselves that the teething troubles would be sorted out and the steamers would stop only when required but as the months went by the quirks of the 'Era' and the 'Autopsy' multiplied. By then all other steam carriages had been taken off the road. But Hancock did not give up easily. In July 1835 he brought out his best and last steam omnibus the 'Automaton'.

The 'Automaton' was larger than the others, being able to carry 22 passengers and was designed to achieve an average speed of 13 m.p.h. On its trial run from London to Romford and back it managed no better than 11 m.p.h. but this was quite sufficient for London streets. Indeed, on one occasion it was driven at top speed down Bow Lane and recorded the incredible speed of 22 m.p.h. Hancock was over the moon. Forgetting his past failures he put pen to paper and announced to the world:

Years of practice have now put all doubts of economy, safety and superiority of steam travelling on common roads at rest when compared with horse travelling; I have now in preparation calculations, founded upon actual practice, which when published, will prove that steam locomotion on common roads is not unworthy of the attention of the capitalist..... Though the reverse has been broadcast rather widely of late by parties who do not desire that this branch of improvement should prosper against the interests of themselves.

The parties against Hancock's branch of improvement were none other than the horse omnibus proprietors. Hancock alleged a dirty tricks campaign on the part of his rivals. He claimed they had sabotaged his operations by covering the roads with stones several inches deep. The inventors of the steamers had claimed that their vehicles would not harm roads, their wheels were wider, they said; no horses' hooves damaged the surface. But there was truth in the accusation. Dance's Gloucester to Cheltenham service had undoubtedly damaged the road surface, and the two foot depth of stones added by the authorities bought an end to the service. Elsewhere in England and Scotland the roads authorities acted likewise. Within months the number of steam services was drastically reduced. To add insult to injury the Government passed many local Turnpike Bills, putting heavy tolls on steam road transport, for example, horse coach 4/-; steam carriage 48/-. This signalled the end. Within a short time all services had failed.

Hancock certainly had a fair crack at the whip (if one can use so equine a phrase about a steam carriage proprietor). No one spread stones in London.The 'Automaton', the best steam-omnibus ever built, was, none the less, a failure. Passengers used it less and less. Hancock struggled on until 1840 but the end came with the enforcement of the Turnpike Acts in London.

6. Brave Names,Wild Races and Bad Manners

While Hancock was struggling, horse-drawn omnibuses prospered financially. Their owners were opening new routes all over London and the surrounding districts. In 1837 there were 14 omnibuses from Blackheath to Charing Cross, 27 from Chelsea to Mile End Gate; 41 from Piccadilly to Blackwall; 19 from Hampstead to Holborn, Charing Cross and the Bank; 17 from The Angel Islington to the Elephant and Castle; and 25 from Edgware Road to the Bank. Other routes ran into the City from Putney, Kew, Richmond, Deptford, Greenwich, Lewisham, Holloway, Highbury, Hornsey, Norwood, Kennington, Dulwich and many more places besides.

It became fashionable to name the various omnibus routes: the *Favorites*, the *Eagles*, the *Wellingtons*, the *King Williams*, the *Marlboroughs*, the *Hopes*, the *Victorians*, the *Emperors*, the *Venuses*, the *Nelsons, Les Dames Blanches* and the *Marquis of Westminster* were all popular routes. However, by the turn of the century only one of these names had survived, the *Favorites*; the others being replaced by the *Atlases*, the *Paragons*, the *Royal Blues*, and the *Times*.

The *Eagles* underwent a metamorphosis to become the *Royal Blues*. Owned by an old busman, John Clark, they were originally painted green and ran from The Compasses at Pimlico to Blackwall via Piccadilly. The story goes that one day an Eagle was passing Hyde Park Corner when it was overtaken by the young Queen Victoria, as yet unmarried, on horseback. Her habit became caught in the door handle and the conductor, Clark himself, immediately freed it. The Queen graciously thanked him for his prompt action and, to mark the occasion, he had that particular omnibus repainted blue and a picture of the Queen painted on the door panel. Eventually he repainted all the buses on that route but the original was the only one to carry a picture of the Queen. Another version of the story makes Clark the driver not conductor. When he saw Her Majesty coming towards him on horseback, he made a great show of pulling out of her way. As the road was partially blocked, this was not easy but, being an old timer, he succeeded. The Queen, noting his efforts, graciously bowed to him as she rode by. No doubt there was some truth in the stories. The Queen's portrait on the door of a bus was pointed out to visitors to London. When the omnibus reached the end of its working life and was scrapped, Clark had the panel removed and framed, and on his death he bequeathed it to his daughter.

The Favorite in the lead. Passengers in the mid 1840s were starting to ride the upper deck, beside and just behind the driver [painting by J. Pollard]

There was friendly rivalry between the omnibus companies. This led to what the old stage-coach drivers had termed the 'go-by' but which in common parlance is know as racing. The chief offenders were the *Favorites* and their great rivals the *Hopes*. The passengers colluded with the drivers in this exciting venture. One omnibus from each company would start from opposite the Angel and go careering at breakneck speed down the City Road to the Bank. This led to accidents and the local authorities offered a reward to anyone giving information that would lead to a conviction. This certainly checked the enthusiasm of the Islington drivers but elsewhere in London racing went on for many years. Another favourite racing track was down Haymarket from Coventry Street. There was a cab-rank in the middle of the road; one omnibus would go one side and the other choose the opposite. It is said that they often collided at the other end. So fond of racing were the passengers, that when damage was done to either vehicle the passengers would nearly always help to foot the bill!

The horses were probably not so enthusiastic, some were in a very poor condition – a disgrace to the city. A story tells of an out-of-work coachman applying for a job as an omnibus driver, his interview went something like this:
"Ever driven a bus before?" asked the proprietor.
"Yes sir, I drove a Kingsland bus."
"Hm. Discharged, I suppose,"
"No sir, I left because I wanted a change."
"How many accidents have you had?"
"None at all sir."
"Smart coachman! Have you let many horses down?"
"Never let one down, sir."
"Get out of my yard," shouted the proprietor,"you're no good to me, I want a man who's had plenty of practice at getting horses up; mine are always falling down."

A coster's cart in trouble with speeding buses. On the left is a 'threepenny' bus, with gents sitting on the top at the front. On the right is an early version of the knifeboard seat (see p. 21) The 3d bus is cited by W. S. Gilbert in Patience *as the height of suburban ordinariness [painting by Eugène Lami]*

If the drivers were popular with the passengers, the conductors were not. The travelling public complained that they were rude to passengers and spent too much time chatting to the drivers, instead of making sure that passengers could catch their eye to alight at the required stop. Another grievance was the way they slammed the door whenever a passenger got in or out. Some passengers complained that conductors stood at the doorway, gazing in at the travellers and polluting the atmosphere with their foul smelling breath – such a complaint today could cause a national bus strike! The 'Cads' as conductors had become known, did not bother

The conductor, or 'Cad', hanging on the strap provided for him to keep his position. He stands on his special platform, placed high enough for him to see the top of the bus.

These arrangements lasted from the earliest days of rooftop passengers until the advent of the large rear platform and proper staircases.

Note the primitive form of ladder behind him – definitely not to be used by ladies!

to keep disreputable types off the omnibuses. One poor old lady had a frightening experience. She entered the omnibus and the door was banged shut behind her with the usual shattering crash.

"Right away, Bill", shouted the conductor to the driver, before the lady had the opportunity to be seated. She was catapulted to the far end of the saloon, falling into the laps of some male passengers. Before she had time to make a timid apology she was verbally assaulted with some of the vilest language imaginable. Horrified at such language, the old lady started to reprove them when she realised that her three villainous looking assailants were convicts – chained together and in the charge of a warder! She shouted to the conductor to stop the omnibus but he was chatting to the driver and did not hear whereupon she opened the door and in her confusion fell into the road. This was enough to interrupt the conversation. The omnibus stopped, the conductor leapt down and insisted that the lady paid her fare. Then the vehicle moved off, leaving the old lady, bruised and still shaking in the middle of the road. It was remarked that some passengers matched the caddish conductors for rudeness.

The Times must have agreed with them; it published the following guide to behaviour on omnibuses:

> 1. Keep your feet off the seats.
> 2. Do not go into a snug corner yourself, and then open the window to admit a nor-wester upon your neighbour's neck.
> 3. Have your money ready when you desire to alight; if your time is not valuable, that of others may be.
> 4. Do not impose on the conductor the necessity of finding change; he is not a banker.
> 5. Sit with your limbs straight, and do not let your legs describe an angle of forty-five, therefore occupying the room of two people,
> 6. Do not spit on the straw, you are not in a hog sty, but in an omnibus, travelling in a country which boasts of refinements.
> 7. Behave respectfully to females, and put not an unprotected lass to blush because she cannot escape from your brutality.
> 8. If you bring a dog, let him be small and confined by string.
> 9. Do not introduce large parcels; an omnibus is not a van.
> 10. Reserve bickering and disputes for the open fields. The sound of your own voice may be music to your own ears, not so perhaps, to those of your companions.
> 11. If you broach politics or religion, speak with moderation; all have an equal right to their opinions, and all have an equal right not to have them wantonly shocked.
> 12. Refrain from affectation and conceited airs. Remember you are riding a distance for sixpence, which, if made in an Hackney Coach would cost you as many shillings; and that should your pride elevate you above plebeian accommodations, your purse should enable you to command aristocratic indulgence.

No matter what was said of some passengers, the behaviour of the conductors went from bad to worse. Much of the blame could be laid at the operators' feet. Not all were as well bred as George Shillibeer; most were ex-drivers or conductors, and, knowing the temptations from first hand experience, they were obsessed with preventing their staff from swindling them. As today, the lack of respect for staff on the part of the management influenced the way the conductors treated the passengers. The inquiry office clerks were no better, often surly and obstinate, as the following story shows:

One afternoon, at 4.20 p.m., a gentleman went into the omnibus office at the George and Blue Boar in Holborn. He asked the clerk if omnibuses went to a certain railway station.

"Yes." was the reply.

"At what hour?" enquired the gentleman

"One hour before each train."

"Then I'm just in time to catch the 5.30."

"It's all down in writing on the board."

The traveller turned to the board and, finding the 5.30 p.m. train entered upon it, he went outside to await the omnibus.

After pacing up and down for a quarter of an hour, with no sign of an omnibus, he went back inside and enquired as to its whereabouts.

"It's gone," the clerk informed him.

"Then it did not start from here, I've been waiting outside since twenty past four."

"What train did you want to catch?"

"The half-past-five, I asked about it before."

"Ho! We ain't got no homnibus to catch that train."

"But my good man, you said that you had one to catch each train."

"I told you it was all down in writing on that there board, and you ought to 'ave seen for yourself. There ain't no homnibus for the 'alf-past-five."

The traveller turned again to the board, and after glancing at it declared angrily, "There's nothing of the kind stated here!"

The clerk pointed to a small cross against the 5.30 p.m. train and said smugly, "This 'ere mark means there ain't no homnibus,"

"Well, how the deuce was I to know that?" asked the gentleman,

"Most gentlemen, when they sees it, asks me what the deuce it means, and I tells 'em."

"But what do the others do?"

The clerk did not deign to reply, and put his full attention to peeling an apple with his pocket knife.

If customer care left something to be desired for regular operators, it was non-existent for pirate omnibuses. These were small fry who competed with respectable operators, overcharging passengers and stopping short of the advertised destination, particularly when their passengers were female, children or foreigners. They were at their worst in Shillibeer's time but plied their trade for seventy years or more. The following story is typical of their mode of operation.

One night in 1836 several passengers from Greenwich for London boarded what they thought was one of Shillibeer's vehicles. Even when full the omnibus did not start, and when the passengers tendered the usual fare of 1/- the conductor with a string of oaths told them the fare that night was 18d. The passengers refused to pay the extra and threatened to report the man for extortion and bad language. Realising a shilling was all he would get he told the driver to start. But in a deserted street in Greenwich the omnibus halted, and the driver and conductor unhitched the horses and disappeared into the darkness. A deputation of the passengers visited Shillibeer the next day, but on learning the number on the omnibus, 588, he was able to assure them it was not one of his.

This was not an isolated incident, and the traveller's only redress was to publish, at his own expense, the number of a suspect vehicle in the paper. It seems extraordinary that authority, while coming down so heavily on responsible operators, did little or nothing to curb such pirates.

7. The Great Exhibition and the Knifeboard

Omnibus operations continued piecemeal until 1851. Companies were in direct competition which led to law suits, the lawyers were kept fully occupied. However, in that year, a group of London omnibus proprietors met at the Duke of Wellington, Bathurst St, Argyle Square, at the suggestion of a Mr. Crawford of the Camden Town Omnibus Association. The meeting decided to introduce new lines, including one from Bayswater to the Bank; twenty new omnibuses from Rock and Gower were ordered. The new venture was an instant success.

Similar groups had sprung up in other areas, the proprietors were realising that there was more profit to be made from cooperation than direct opposition. The associations shared management and office expenses, they worked on improved timetables and encouraged individual members to stick to them. Conductors were now engaged and controlled by the secretary of the association, while the owners provided the vehicles and horses. The associations were known as 'Times', each member owning as many Times as he owned buses, so an association with 20 Times might have one owner with three buses, another with seven, and a third with ten.

It was the year of The Great Exhibition; London was full of foreign tourists, the omnibuses were full – and so were the conductors' pockets! Ever resourceful, the conductors found a new way of diddling foreigners. Every morning they armed themselves with small change. The unfortunate passenger giving half a crown for a fourpenny fare was given two sixpences and a couple of halfpennies change. He was left still scratching his head, trying to work out if the sum was correct when the omnibus drove off.

On one such journey, there was a dispute between a Frenchman and an Italian. The Italian pulled up the window whereupon the Frenchman promptly opened it again. The Italian retaliated, the Frenchman parried only to be thwarted again. At last the Frenchman broke the window and, much to the amusement of his fellow passengers, said,

"Now, monsieur, you can hev zee vindow up if you like!"

By this time, of course, Shillibeer had abandoned omnibuses, but his place was taken by Thomas Tilling, a name that was to be associated with buses for a century or more. Tilling was a self-made man. He started with a single horse, a grey. In four years time he started an omnibus service between Peckham and Oxford Circus, calling it the *Times*. Within a short time he had 24 *Times* omnibuses on the road and, unlike other proprietors, his horses were so well cared for that his were the fastest omnibuses in London. At first he would use only greys but eventually he had to relent, through sheer weight of business. He ran 160 omnibuses and a stud of 4,000. His interests extended to coaches, cabs and wedding carriages and on Derby Day he would have as many as 200 horses working to the course. Although he was present at Epsom for 30 years he never once saw the race run, indeed it was fair to assume that he was not a betting man. On one occasion on returning to Peckham, having been at Epsom all day he asked his clerk which horse had won!

He treated his employees as well as he treated his horses. He tolerated neither swearing nor gambling but his men held him in high esteem, staying with the company for many years. As time passed and business grew he ordered that a photograph should be taken of every man in his employ for twenty years or more, to be hung in the main office. The walls were covered with photographs of long serving employees, some, eventually, with as many as fifty years service. When he died in 1893 each one of his employees felt a personal sense of loss.

In 1846 advertisements appeared inside omnibuses for the first time. Mr. Frederick Marriot, of 335 The Strand, gave one of his omnibuses the name 'Publicity Omnibus'. Whether or not Mr. Marriot derived much personal benefit for his idea, it caught on quickly. Soon advertisement revenue became nearly as necessary as it was to newspapers and magazines. The newspapers resented the competition. One eminent paper objected to the bad taste of omnibuses displaying a money lender's advertisement. Needless to say, the proprietor of the omnibus company wrote to the Editor pointing out that the illustrious paper was being inconsistent, carrying on its pages as it did four such advertisements. Not surprisingly the letter was not published!

Every now and again someone would have a bright idea for attracting more passengers. In 1851 a new patent omnibus was put on the road. Each passenger had a compartment entirely to himself, like a private box at a theatre; this idea was short lived but another fared better. The 'Knifeboard' omnibus carried nine extra passengers outside. They were seated on a narrow foot-high bench running the length of the omnibus. These seats were very popular with the public but the police declared them to be dangerous. And dangerous they were; the passengers clambered up on to the roof from the right of the door and sat facing the road. There were no near-side seats but occasionally conductors allowed passengers to sit with their legs dangling down over the rail in front of the windows, having first been warned that they would be charged for damaged windows – glass was more fragile in those days. The appeal of open-top buses remains today, as anyone with small children can testify.

The first recorded use of the term 'knifeboard' (so called from the seats' ressemblance to the domestic knife sharpener) dates fom 1852. A clerestory roof bus with seating lengthways on the top had appeared in 1847. Earlier in the 1840s two rows of upper-deck passengers had sat beside and behind the driver. By the end of the 1850s knifeboard seating with two rows of passengers back to back was in general use; examples of the type survived until the end of the century.

Early examples of the knifeboard seat:

Left: the first, built by Adams of Fairfield Works, Bow, for the Economic Conveyance Company in 1847. A dozen years on their use was spreading.

On the right are two London General types, the upper one being probably slightly later for the toppers are less 'stove pipe' in fashion, and the cad is notably smarter.

The advent of the General is described overleaf

8. Another French Invasion: the General

Neither improvements in bus design nor the presence of the associations led to any marked improvement in services, for competition continued to breed ups and downs in fares, and other unfortunate consequences. This was noted by the French financier M. Jacques Orsi, one of the promotors of the Compagnie Générale des Omnibus, which fused the 10 Parisian omnibus companies into one monopoly, by imperial decree, in February 1855. Still in Paris, in December of that year, Orsi set up a Société en Commandite (limited liability) entitled Compagnie Générale des Omnibus de Londres, to take over and reorganise as many as possible of the existing London firms. Apart from Orsi there were four French directors and three English. In some quarters their project met with even more hostility than Shillibeer's French predilictions, and, deciding against adopting the title of the London Omnibus Company — as a firm by that name had already failed — they simply translated their French title into English: the London General Omnnibus Company. Further to allay suspicion about French origins they took on four of the leading omnibus proprietors as managers. Doubtless a sound notion from the operational aspect too!

On the morning of January 7th, 1856, Wilson's omnibuses, the *Favorites,* emerged from their Islington and Holloway depots emblazoned with the addition of the words 'London General Omnibus Company'. Wilson was the biggest proprietor to sell out. His concern boasted 50 omnibuses, 500 horses and employed 180 men. Mr. Leonard Willing, the oldest established proprietor, also sold out. His fleet which served the Stoke Newington, Kingsland and Dalston lines, comprised 22 omnibuses and 200 horses, employing 70 men.

Within a few days other lines passed into French hands giving it a fleet of 198 vehicles, 1940 horses with 670 men. The new company also bought out Messrs. Bennet, Breech, Chancellor, Clark, Forge, Fox, Hartley, Hawtry, Hinckly, Horne, Hunt, Johnson, Kerrison, Macnamara, Martin, Proome, Seale, Smith, Wenn Westopp, Williams and Woodford. Two famous proprietors, Birch and Tilling, resolutely refused to be taken over, then or later.

The company had hoped to run 500 omnibuses, but for the time being they had to be content with 300. By the end of 1856 they had 450 in daily use with more in reserve, and early the following year they had built more than 50 new omnibuses and rebuilt 120 old ones.

Before the year was out the company was introducing new ideas. One such innovation was known as 'correspondence'. Already successful in Paris, the idea was to allow passengers to travel from any one part of London to any other for a flat fare of 6d. They could board an omnibus near their home and then transfer to another which went nearer to their destination. It is not clear whether conductors advised passengers to transfer or whether they simply leapt from one omnibus to another! Despite its success corresponding was discontinued in London, perhaps it became less financially viable and more difficult to operate as more and more companies sold out to the London General.

> Any Passenger desiring
> CORRESPONDENCE, must ask
> for a Ticket at the time of paying his fare
> The Ticket will be available only
> by the next Omnibus in which
> there is room, after its
> arrival at the Office.

Another innovation, still everyday practice in France, was the purchase of prepaid tickets in packets of ten, with a 10% discount. On the first day 10,000 tickets were sold by the company's Strand office alone. This scheme was popular with shops. Linen drapers bought thousands of tickets, selling them to their customers at a discount, or giving them as a reward to high spending customers – marketing gimmicks are not unique to the twentieth century! For some reason this practice did not seem to suit London as well as it did Paris; prepayment was abandoned by the directors.

Large scale operation brought other benefits. At first omnibuses retained their original colours with matching wheels in all colours of the rainbow – red, green, brown, white, yellow and chocolate – but the directors soon saw that a uniform wheel colour would save greatly on the number of spares stocked so all wheels were painted yellow.

In the autumn of 1858 it was decided to convert the French company to an English limited liability company. The London General Omnibus Company Limited was registered on November 16th, 1858, with a nominal capital of £700,000, divided into 175,000 shares of £4 each. With the stigma of the French connection removed the Company went from strength to strength, as will be revealed later in these pages.

Cad's vocabulary
'Ste-'ank   City – Bank
'nich! 'wich   Greenwich, Woolwich
'ngton!   Paddington or Islington
'mpton   Brompton
'smith!   Hammersmith
A Hangel   passenger from Islington
A Helephant   passenger from Newington
A Blue Boar   passenger from Holborn
A Saracen   passenger from Snow-Hill
Plenty of room ma'am   16 inside

left:
THE TEST OF GALLANTRY
Conductor: "WILL ANY GENT BE SO GOOD AS FOR TO TAKE THIS YOUNG LADY IN HIS LAP?"
Leech, 1845

right:
Conductor: "'OLD TIGHT, LADY!"
Fare: "'OO ARE YOU CALLIN' A OLD TIGHT LADY? IMPIDENT YOUNG FELLER!"
Bernard Partridge, 1898

left: Jones (singi
"ADDIO LEON
['Bus suddenly
Cad (with asper
Driver: "WHY;
Cad: "GO ALO
A-HOLLERIN'"
[Jones *tacet* for t

A GIRLISH IGNORANCE

Lady Hildegarde, who is studing the habits of the democracy, determines to travel by omnibus.
Lady H: "CONDUCTOR, TELL THE DRIVER TO GO TO NO 104 BERKELEY SQUARE, AND THEN HOME!"
Everard Hopkins, 1901

Cartoons from Punch *depicting:*
top left: an omnibus of the 1840s with fare painted on the panel and a banner showing the destination
lower left: an early knifeboard type, 1858
centre and right: buses with proper stairs, at the turn of the century. Note Lady Hildegarde's conductor's bell punch

9. Kindness to Horses, Flying the Flag and Frustrating the Fiddlers

The horses had to work hard for their living. After a frost or rainfall the streets of London became dangerous for horses pulling a heavy load. They stumbled and fell. Horse lovers were saddened by the pitiful sight of a horse struggling to its feet again. Nowhere was so bad as Holborn Hill. For years people living nearby complained of the hardship to horses. Eventually the City Corporation put an end to the horses' plight by building a viaduct. The foundation stone was laid on June 3rd, 1867 and the viaduct was officially opened by Queen Victoria on Saturday, November 6th, 1869. At nine on the following Monday the barriers were lifted and the viaduct was opened to the public. There was a mad rush as every driver vied to give his vehicle the honour of being first across. The honour went to a *City Atlas* omnibus of the London General Omnibus Company. Tommy Grayson, its driver was cheered on enthusiastically by his passengers. To commemorate the event Tommy Grayson's regular passengers presented him with a new whip, bearing a suitably inscribed plaque. Some also wanted a photograph of the memorable occasion. Grayson obliged; he had a photograph printed bearing the legend:

> **First over Holborn Viaduct**
> **on November 8th, 1869**
> **at 9 am**
> **Copies may be had of driver**
> **Thomas Grayson**
> **1 Victoria Place**
> **Kilburn**

The whole print run was sold in no time at 6d a copy, most bought by residents of St. John's Wood who lived on his regular route. Some were bought by fellow crew members, who christened him Viaduct Tommy. Even after he was retired the people of Kilburn delighted in pointing him out to strangers.

Not everyone was pleased with the viaduct. There was honest employment to be had from putting skids on vehicles before they started down the hill. One skidman used by omnibus men could earn between 12/- and 15/- a day. The horses' gain was the skidmen's loss.

On April 7th, 1881 a new company started operating. The London Road Car Company Limited had a capital of £200,000 financed by 20,000 £10 shares. The original road cars had an entrance at the front and proper stairs, on both sides, immediately behind the driver; but this arrangement led to several accidents, when

Below left: Tommy Grayson with the first vehicle to cross Holborn Viaduct–
a knifeboard omnibus, fitted with decency boards bearing advertisements
Below: Cooling the horses in hot weather. c 1900

passengers alighting from moving buses encountered the rear wheel. The buses were therefore rebuilt, with platform and a single staircase at the back. At the same time the knifeboard seat was replaced by lateral 'garden' seats on either side of a gangway. This design was subsequently adopted by most operators. With the advent of the stairs the upper deck became accessible in theory – and later in practice – to the ladies, and to prevent their ankles being gazed upon by passers-by, the sides of the upper deck were fitted with 'decency boards' which also proved a useful position for advertisements.

The Road Car Company soon had 455 omnibuses on the road, each one sporting a Union Jack on the front of the upper deck, to prove that the Company was British. Since most people had probably forgotten the French origins of the General this ploy may have served better as a route identifier than as an essay in patriotism.

Another omnibus concern with a famous visible trade mark was the Metropolitan Railway Company, whose omnibuses, operating in connection with its train services, were graced at the front by a large red umbrella. It possibly afforded a bit of protection to one or two passengers, but was more useful as an eye-catcher. Another eye-catching feature was conductors in uniform, quite unique in the horse bus era. The Metropolitan apparently had no statutory powers to operate omni-

The driver of a Road Car omnibus, with the Union Jack at the masthead.
This is a 'garden seat' vehicle; the overhang of the upper deck is conspicuous.
Note also the driver's 'apron' initialled L.R.C.Cº.

buses, but this was evidently no deterrent; umbrellas and uniformed conductors remained conspicuous for several decades.

Another innovation by the Road Car Company was the ticket system. This had been satisfactorily used on the tramways which were starting to spread round London in the 1870s, but had not yet been tried on omnibuses. Eventually it proved enormously successful, but to begin with, when other companies applied it, it was not regarded with any enthusiasm by the crews. The 'perks' of a conductor were generally divided not only with the driver but also with the stablemen, so the conductors adopted various means of fiddling the tickets. Sometimes they colluded with passengers and no ticket was issued (a practice not unknown today!) Sometimes they reissued old tickets retrieved fom the floor. Some conductors would mangle ticket rolls under the wheels of omnibus and say they had been damaged in an accident, others would throw them away and report them stolen, the more militant of their number even bragged that they gave them to their children to play with.

The obvious solution was to employ inspectors. The inspectors were known to crewmen as 'Jumpers', the conductors took it as personal affront that someone should check whether they issued tickets, some even assaulted the inspectors but the Police Court magistrates soon taught them the error of their ways. Some complaints were justified. As one conductor said "We have to punch tickets in the dark,

The Omnibus conductor at the turn of the century. Compare him – and the back of the omnibus – with the Cad in his perilous position, p. 16. Note he still does not wear uniform

A Metropolitan Railways omnibus with umbrella at the front, heading up Regent Street (which was entirely rebuilt in the 1920s) This large vehicle probably started life with a knifeboard in the 1880s and was converted to garden seats in the 1890s

then a Jumper comes on with his electric light to see if we have punched them in the right section."

"Perhaps they'll fix electric lights on top of the omnibus before long," said a helpful passenger.

" 'Ope not, Guv'ner," replied the conductor with a twinkle in his eye, "Shouldn't get no more two-bob bits for pennies, if they did that!"

Soon the travelling public was familiar with ticket inspectors, but very few people were aware of the private inspector. These plain clothes inspectors were nicknamed 'Spots' or 'Wrong'uns' by the busmen, who could never be sure if a passenger was genuine. The man in evening dress who got on in the Strand after the theatres had closed could be a Spot, so too could be the man with a bag of tools on an early morning run. And even a well-dressed young lady boarding outside a smart ladies outfitters might not be all she seemed! Could her interest in the good looking conductor and his manoeuvres be inspired by something more than natural interest in the opposite sex? What about the distinguished retired officer getting on at Piccadilly; could he be supplementing his pension? And how did these impostors

Another Metropolitan Railway omnibus, this time of more modern design. The umbrellas were red and inscribed 'Metropolitan Railway'. The scene is Piccadilly Circus

feel as they faced the advertisement for Sapolio, bearing Lady Macbeth's exhortation "Out, out damned Spot"?

The fear of Spots must have had repercussions on some passengers. Woe betide the passenger who peered too closely at the conductor's badge, who watched the conductor at his ticket machine out of idle curiosity! One day an immaculately dressed woman was suspected of being a Spot. The conductor signalled his suspicion to the driver who, when the lady wanted to disembark, chose for her the biggest, dirtiest puddle he could find!

Smartly dressed ladies might be 'Spots' in disguise and, as such, a menace to conductors. Or they might be something quite different, a menace to passengers. This young woman must have a false sleeve in her muff – look what her right hand is doing!

The duties of the inspectors in the early days had not been so onerous, they had merely to distinguish 'Long' passengers (1/-) from 'Shorts' (6d), a relatively easy task which could yet yield surprises; one operator received reports from his Spot that a certain omnibus had carried 12 Longs and 16 Shorts, but the conductor paid in fares for 14 Longs and 17 Shorts! The proprietor enlisted a relation, unknown to the busmen, to spy on the Spot. The spy's account tallied with that of the Spot; they both agreed that the conductor was paying in too much! The spy then rode two journeys without the Spot and the mystery was solved. On these occasions the conductor paid in only three quarters of the fares. He confessed that he had bribed the operator's clerk to identify the Spot for him. Had he not overcompensated for his dishonesty on journeys when he knew himself to be watched, he might have continued the fraud for years!

Despite an attempt by operators to appease the conductors' grievances by giving a wage rise of 2/- a day, matters finally came to a head in a strike. On the night of Saturday, May 6th, 1891 large meetings were held in many parts of London showing much support for action. Of course the men could not openly admit that this was because of their loss of 'perks', so they attributed it to the fact that they were expected to work 15 to 17 hours per day. The strike began the next day, and even the Road Car men, who on the face of it had nothing to lose, joined in. Some crews stayed loyal to their employers but were thwarted by pickets of angry strikers at the stable gates. For a week the streets of London looked strangely deserted save for a few pirate buses whose operators contributed to the strike fund since it was in their interests to keep the strike going.

If the hours of omnibus men were long and the conditions hard, the training was fairly rigorous too, in the latter half of the 19th century. The white bearded gentleman seen here testing cab and omnibus drivers doubtless struck terror into the hearts of many potential candidates, especially as he was a representative of the Chief Commissioner of New Scotland Yard

The omnibus is a knifeboard seat type without decency board, already archaic at the date of the photograph and presumably used exclusively for training

Most men returned to work on Sunday May 14th, upon an agreement of a daily maximum of 12 hours work. A few, almost a century ahead of their time, decided they would set up their own company, the London Cooperative Omnibus Company, with the conductors, coachmen and horse keepers all to be shareholders. The company was launched with a single omnibus adorned with a broom to signify the intention of sweeping all other buses off the road, but there never was another bus, the company itself was swept into oblivion.

In truth, the 'perks' system belonged to the long gone stage coach era when box seat fares went to the driver and guard. The crews of the 1890s had to come to terms with progress. Despite fears that tickets would cost more to operate than they recouped, the London General alone is said to have saved £100,000 a year after their introduction! By 1893 the Bell Punch ticket system was in general use on the

The streets of London were usually thronged with omnibuses as witness these views of Fleet Street Corner (Ludgate Circus).....

L.G.O.C. Ten years later the annual consumption of paper for L.G.O.C. tickets was in excess of 750 tons!

Traffic was also a problem. As far back as 1867 the Metropolitan Streets Act had forbidden buses from dropping off or picking up passengers on whichever side of the road the passenger chose. There was to be no more pulling of strings on the driver's arms, only the nearside was permissible. Thirty years later, with traffic conditions much worse, Parliament proposed a Bill giving the police powers to divert omnibuses to relieve congestion. This aroused indignation in both the omnibus men and their passengers. M.P.s were bombarded with letters asking them to vote against the measure. In June 1899, Sir J. Blundell Maple M.P. presented the Home Secretary with a petition of more than 100,000 signatures against the Bill. It was withdrawn on October 14th of that year and for three days busmen displayed

.....and the junction of Cannon Street and Queen Victoria Street. So they must have looked very strange during the strike

Sir Blundell Maple's racing colours on their whips and bell cords as a mark of gratitude.

At Christmas many whips and bell-pulls were decked out in the Rothschild racing colours. The Rothschild firm gave Christmas boxes to busmen; a brace of pheasants was not uncommon. This curious custom was said to have originated with the good deed for the day of a busman many years previously. One day the traffic had been stopped in Park Lane to clear the road for a royal carriage. An omnibus conductor, one Benjamin West by name, noticed a lady of the Rothschild family trying to cross the road. The road was jammed with cabs and omnibuses and the horses were becoming restless. West jumped down from his step and escorted the lady across. She sent her page to enquire his name and rewarded him. An apocryphal story perhaps, but bankers riding daily to work by omnibus no doubt included the busmen in their list of folk to be tipped at Christmas!

Christmas in an omnibus. The worthy fellow consuming his Yuletide fare in L.G.O.C. 383 is perhaps a beneficiary of Rothschild generosity, and certainly the envy of the passengers

10. Kindness to Drivers; and Other Statistics

In the latter days of the horse omnibus conductors were generally respectable and intelligent. After just one year's service they could earn 6/- a day. Among their ranks were former clerks, shop assistants and non-commissioned army officers. An Oxford graduate was a conductor on a West End omnibus for many years, so also was a former city man who, when made bankrupt, chose to become a conductor on the very route he had taken to his former workplace. The drivers were not generally so bright although, at 8/- a day, they earned more than conductors. Perhaps their familiarity with horses led to uncouth behaviour, albeit tinged with witticisms:

"Now then, short weight, hurry up," to the driver of a coal cart, or,"Got a bit of freehold there?" to another omnibus outstaying his welcome at a stop. Or again, to a would-be passenger hailing them on their journey back to the depot at midnight, "Not tonight, Sir, we have the rest of the evening to ourselves."

For some, high wages fuelled an expensive interest in horse racing – many a driver who started at 21 retired not a penny richer than he had started – and ended his days in the workhouse. The plight of aged busmen did not go unnoticed. A Mr. Morris Abrahams had always shown an interest in the well being of his local busmen and, when asked to contribute to one fallen on hard times, gave so generously that he was invited to make the presentation himself. In so doing he realised that his gift would merely postpone poverty for a few months. He suggested

Midnight; the last omnibus

starting a superannuation fund, promising both to support it himself and also to find the neccessary money to set it up. At the first meeting 650 busmen were present and £40 was subscribed on the spot. Mr. Abrahams presented the fund with £250 from Messrs. Barnato. Before long the scheme had 1,300 members and reserves of £3,200. Mr. Abrahams was elected president and Mr. Alfred Rothschild vice-president and the fund was supported by the Duke of Cambridge, the Duke of Westminster, the Earl of Crewe, Lord Rosebery, and other members of both Houses of Parliament. The fund gave 15/- a week for life to any busman incapacitated in the course of duty. The first recipient was 'Fat' Smith, a well-known driver on the Kilburn to Victoria route. The respect and support commanded by the London crewmen seems difficult to imagine today. Even the theatrical profession played its part; Mr. George Alexander lent his theatre for a matinée and actors and actresses gave freely of their services, performing to a packed house from 2.30 pm to 6 o'clock. The old busmen went on to the stage at the end to bow their thanks. Further support was promised by the thespians.

It was many years before Mr. Abrahams would accept any reward himself, but at last, on 27th June, 1901, he bowed to the busmen's determination to thank him.

At the Holborn Restaurant he was presented with a silver model of an omnibus, with the figures of Jim Parry, an eighty-one year old driver, and conductor, J. Baker, 'Sailor Jack', faithfully depicted.

The turn of the century and the end of the Victorian era marked the apogee of horse bus development. The design of vehicles had been perfected with regard to both the weight that horses could reasonably haul and to passengers' comfort and convenience, and a dense and intensive network of routes was operated. The L.G.O.C. built its own omnibuses at its works at Highbury but the omnibuses of other companies were equally creditable. The vehicles themselves cost about £150 and lasted up to 12 years. They were renovated each year, just before the police inspection. The licensing authorities had two plates issued on alternate years so that constables could tell at a glance whether the omnibus held a current licence. The licences cost £2 a year with 15/- tax on top.

At the end of their working life some omnibuses were sold at auction, being bought for summer houses, workman's sheds, dressing rooms for cricket clubs or refreshment bars. The London General Omnibus Company, however, preferred to burn its old vehicles.

The golden age of the horse omnibus, at Hyde Park Corner, above, and the Royal Exchange, left: in this view nearly all the gents are looking south

The L.G.O.C.'s half year figures for the period ending 30th June, 1901 – not quite half a century after the Compagnie Générale started – showed that 101,109,572 passengers had been carried 15,969,602 miles in its 1,373 omnibuses. The omnibuses were pulled by 16,714 horses who consumed 25,299 tons of oats, maize and peas! The total number of omnibuses licensed in London that year was 3,736.

Most omnibuses were drawn by pairs of horses, though a few express services (much favoured by regular City patrons) boasted three or even four. A pair of horses might work up to four or five hours a day. Generally speaking an omnibus would have five changes of horse, or six on hilly routes, so up to twelve horses would be needed for each omnibus. Therefore, in round figures, there must have been some 40,000 omnibus horses in London. Most omnibus horses were Canadian. They were bought for around £30 as five to eight-year olds and they were worked in slowly over two or three months. After five years on the omnibuses they were auctioned off, usually bought by farmers. Some farmers were known to sell them back to unsuspecting omnibus proprietors after a spell of country air had restored their 'straight legs'.

Feeding the animals was a tremendous business, as can be seen from the London General's forage figures quoted above, and there was a constant string of carts taking horse fodder in and horse manure out from the stables. Stables were spread all over London, some of the L.G.O.C.'s quarters housing 600 horses — some of them so far outside London that after the 1896 gold rush the busmen nicknamed them the Klondyke!

Above is a red Favorite; these knifeboard-seat vehicles drawn by three horses abreast carried 48 passengers.

On the left is another, hastening towards the City. They were so large that they were barred from City streets after 10 a.m.

Below is a Times (Thomas Tilling) express omnibus, a normal vehicle but with double the horse power

Such a vast supply of horses was seen as a potential goldmine for national defence purposes. Omnibus horses were put on a reserve list, the Government paying 10/- a year for this privilege. During the Boer War many horses were called up, and the proprietors paid an average of £60. The loss of so many horses played havoc with timetables and many services were reduced drastically.

As is the case in any transport system much work went on behind the scenes, and the omnibus stable yards were a hive of activity, particularly at night. At 10 p.m. the first omnibus would arrive back at the yard; the horses would be led to the stables, groomed and fed. The night men were known as 'Washers'; they cleaned and brushed out the vehicles inside and out and polished the brass, hard work, particularly if it had been a wet day. The vehicles had to be ready for inspection by coach builders by 5 a.m., any defect being repaired swiftly. The veterinary surgeons inspected the horses declaring them fit for service or ordering them to be rested. By 7 a.m. the omnibuses were ready for service again. The drivers arrived, carrying whip and rug, and the conductors came, bearing bell-punch and tickets. Together with their first pair of horses they set out for another day on the busy streets of London.

Right: Traffic congestion in Leman Street, Whitechapel, a huge basket is perched perilously on the rear canopy of the omnibus
Below: The corner of Tottenham Court Road

Below: Kensington High Street. In the foreground is the upper deck of a Road Car omnibus, with its Union Jack, and another Road Car can be seen beyond the policeman

London Bridge rush hour

11. The End of an Era

Shillibeer had been right to say that the omnibus could compete with the railways. Steam railways had put the stage coaches out of business in the second quarter of the nineteenth century and there had been fears that the steam underground of the 1860s would threaten the omnibuses. Instead, the directors of the District and Metropolitan Railways themselves complained of unfair competition from the omnibus! London's changing economy, from small workshops to large factories and offices, ensured that both railways and omnibuses not only survived but thrived. Passenger transport was rapidly expanding to reflect changing lifestyles.

In the 1890s the electric underground railway repeated the threat. The Central London Railway (Twopenny Tube) which opened in 1900 and ran between Shepherd's Bush and the Bank, rivalled the L.G.O.C.'s monopoly on this route. Bus travel was considerably more expensive at 5d and at first the L.G.O.C. switched buses from this route to more lucrative ones. But it was soon necessary to reinstate them; within a few months more omnibuses were running than in pre-Tube days. If the tubes had deprived omnibuses of long-distance passengers, and even on occasion left them dependent upon income from advertising revenue, they probably brought a huge increase in short-stage passengers. The threat to the horse bus did not come from underground.

It came instead from two factors, the repeal of the Road Locomotive Act and, surprising for us to imagine in these days, from the anti-pollution lobby.

The earliest development of steam omnibuses had been frustrated by high turnpike charges. Subsequent essays in steam traction were severely hampered by the Road Locomotive Act of 1865 requiring a man with a red flag to walk in front of a mechanically propelled vehicle which must not exceed 2 m.p.h. in towns or 4 m.p.h. in the country. But now there was the political will for change. London's

The youth with the package the perambulator appears his head smacked by the plank.... *hotly pursued by the maid with in the imminent risk of having*

This scene at King's Cross includes a horse tram. These were never serious rivals to the omnibus for they were not allowed to penetrate the streets of inner London

The bicycle was no rival either, its only use at that date being for the weekend exercise of sporting gentlemen.... and the occasional even more sporting lady

At the turn of the century the horse reigned supreme...but here a dog gets right of way from a kindly bobby

streets were horrendously polluted by horse manure. In 1896 the Road Locomotive Act was repealed, clearing the way for the development of the motor omnibus. The horse omnibus could not hope to compete with the motor omnibus. Motor buses required one engine instead of twelve horses, gaseous effluent from petrol seemed infinitely preferable to solid effluent from livestock.

Proprietors of horse-drawn omnibuses were often accused of a natural bias against mechanical omnibuses but this was unlikely, so much capital and land was tied up in horses and stabling that the potential benefits of horse-less omnibuses could not be ignored. However, it would have been foolish to invest capital in untried inventions, so first of all only a few bold inventors chanced their reputation and their livelihood in putting their contraptions on the road.

One such man, Radcliffe Ward, managed even before the repeal of the red flag

Passengers liked the fresh air on the top deck ... but it wasn't quite so fresh behind the smokers!

Act to obtain a Metropolitan Police licence to run an electric omnibus which reached speeds of 7 or 8 m.p.h. in 1889, but only on trial trips; it never entered service. Radcliffe Ward was back in 1897 with the London Electric Omnibus Company, and their 10-seater made demonstration runs from Marble Arch to Notting Hill Gate. It did not carry fare-paying passengers, and if it had they might have complained of the lack of outside seats. London travellers of that date liked the fresh air of the upper deck.

In 1899 the Motor Omnibus Syndicate Ltd. produced a steam omnibus, a double decker on a Gillett steam lorry chassis, and later in the same year the London Steam Omnibus Co. Ltd. changed its name to the Motor Traction Co. Ltd. and on October 9th started a 26-seater petrol engine Daimler between Kennington Park and Victoria. Painted white trimmed with blue, it had a typical horse bus body, but no horses! Instead the driver was on lower deck level with a canopy over his head

But you can't really blame them for smoking on top when a resourceful cove in Piccadilly Circus sells them matches from a pole!

The last L.G.O.C. horse bus completes its final run on October 25th 1911

and a great snout in front of him to house the mechanical horse power.

Though the horse bus men delighted to mock at the frequent breakdowns of these pioneers, the Motor Traction Company kept going for over a year. Nevertheless, at the actual turn of the century, December 31st, 1900, there was no motor bus operating regularly in London.

Thereafter they kept coming in ones and twos – steam, electric or petrol, frequently unsuccessful, until 1905, when the numbers rose from 20 to 200. By 1908, when the L.G.O.C. amalgamated with the Road Car and the Vanguard, there were 1,000. In 1910 the L.G.O.C. licensed 1,142 horse omnibuses and exactly the same number of motor buses.

1910 also saw the introduction of the L.G.O.C.'s B-type, a motor omnibus designed with the experience of the best bits of the previous disasters. It proved an enormous success and nearly 3,000 were built...

...and so the last L.G.O.C. horse omnibus ran on October 25th, 1911, between London Bridge and Moorgate.

Tilling, Birch and some others continued to operate, though numbers halved each year, and then, on August 4th, 1914, the last horses were requisitioned by the military, and the horse omnibus along with a whole way of life was gone forever.